M000198505

The Penguin

by Jesse Tanner

SCHOOL PUBLISHERS

Cover Harcourt Index; 3 (t) ©Graham Robertson/Auscape International; (b) ©Telescope; 4 ©Graham Robertson/Auscape International; 5 ©John Hoelscher /ANT Photo Library/; 6 Harcourt Index; 7 ©Murray Price/ANT Photo Library; 8 ©Colin Blobel/ANT Photo Library; 9 ©Manfred Thonig/ Photolibrary.com; 10 ©Colin Blobel/ANT Photo Library; 11 ©Bryan & Cherry Alexander/Photolibrary. com; 12 ©Norbert Wu/Photolibrary.com; 13–14 Harcourt Index

Printed in Mexico

ISBN 10: 0-15-350442-0
ISBN 13: 978-0-15-350442-6

Ordering Options
ISBN 10: 0-15-350332-7 (Grade 2 Below-Level Collection)
ISBN 13: 978-0-15-350332-0 (Grade 2 Below-Level Collection)
ISBN 10: 0-15-357451-8 (package of 5)
ISBN 13: 978-0-15-357451-1 (package of 5)

2 3 4 5 6 7 8 9 10   050   15 14 13 12 11 10 09 08 07

Emperor Penguins

Antarctica

Emperor penguins live in icy
Antarctica. Although they are birds,
they cannot fly.

January

Summer in Antarctica is from December to March. Emperor penguins eat juicy fish from the cold, blue sea. They make a long trip over the ice to their nesting site. During the trip, there is nothing to eat.

May

Now it is late fall. The penguins have reached their nesting site. They crowd together to keep warm. The sea below them is sealed with ice.

June

It is winter. The female penguin has found her mate. She lays one egg. Now she will disappear from the nesting site. She goes back to the sea to find food.

egg

When she is away, the male rests the egg on his feet. This keeps it off the cold ice. He carefully looks after the egg for sixty-six days.

July and August

The penguin chick hatches. The chick keeps warm under its father's feathers. It stands on his feet.

Finally, the female returns with food for the chick. The male then leaves to find food.

December and January

It is now spring. For three weeks, the female feeds her chick. Then the male returns to help her.

The chicks stay in groups. There
is always the danger that sea birds
will attack the young chicks.

It is summer again. The chicks have
grown. They begin to get new adult feathers.
Soon, their parents will leave them, and they
will learn to care for themselves.

Growing Up

When the chicks are four or five months old, their parents leave them. The chicks learn to swim and to hunt.

When the penguins are four to six years old, they find mates. These young penguins will follow the same pattern of life as their parents.

Think Critically

1. How many days does the male penguin look after the egg?

2. How do the photographs of the penguins help you to understand what it is like to live in Antarctica?

3. What does the female penguin do in June?

4. Why is it important that both penguin parents care for the penguin chick?

5. What fact about the penguins did you find most interesting? Why?

 Science

Make a Time Line Write down the months of the year in the order they are mentioned in the book. Under each month or group of months, draw a picture of something the penguin does at that time of the year.

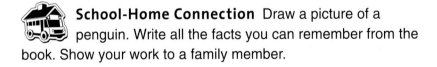 **School-Home Connection** Draw a picture of a penguin. Write all the facts you can remember from the book. Show your work to a family member.

Word Count: 296 (298 with words in graphics)